Figure Skating

BY LAURA HAMILTON WAXMAN

AMICUS HIGH INTEREST • AMICUS INK

Amicus High Interest and Amicus Ink are imprints of Amicus
P.O. Box 1329, Mankato, MN 56002
www.amicuspublishing.us

Library of Congress Cataloging-in-Publication Data
Names: Waxman, Laura Hamilton, author.
Title: Figure skating / by Laura Hamilton Waxman.
Description: Mankato, Minnesota : Amicus High Interest,
[2018] | Series: Winter Olympic Sports | Includes
webography and index. | Audience: Grades: 4 to 6.
Identifiers: LCCN 2016036532 (print) | LCCN 2016039797
(ebook) | ISBN 9781681511481 (library binding) | ISBN
9781681521794 (paperback) | ISBN 9781681512389
(eBook) | ISBN 9781681512389 (pdf)
Subjects: LCSH: Figure skating–Competitions–Juvenile literature.
| Figure skating–Juvenile literature. | Winter Olympics–
Juvenile literature. | Winter sports–Juvenile literature.
Classification: LCC GV850.223 .W39 2018 (print) | LCC
GV850.223 (ebook) | DDC 796.91/2–dc23
LC record available at https://lccn.loc.gov/2016036532

Editor: Wendy Dieker
Series Designer: Kathleen Petelinsek
Book Designer: Aubrey Harper
Photo Researchers: Aubrey Harper and Holly Young

Photo Credits: PCN Photography / Alamy Stock Photo cover,
18; Aflo Co. Ltd. / Alamy Stock Photo 5, 14; AP Photo / Lionel
Cironneau 6; Goh Chai Hin / AFP / Getty Images 9; Paul
Kitagaki Jr. / ZUMA Press, Inc. / Alamy 10; Tribune Content
Agency LLC / Alamy 13, 20-21, 26, 28-29; Adrian Dennis /
AFP / Getty Images 17; Yutaka / Aflo Co. Ltd. / Alamy Stock
Photo 22; Matthew Stockman / Getty Images 25

Printed in the United States of America

HC 10 9 8 7 6 5 4 3 2 1
PB 10 9 8 7 6 5 4 3 2 1

Table of Contents

Going for Gold

The crowd sits on the edges of their seats. They watch a skater glide and spin. They cheer when she jumps off the ice. They gasp as she twirls through the air.

The Winter Olympics happens every four years. The world's best skaters come together. They skate hard. They dream big. They all want a chance to win a gold medal.

Adelina Sotnikova, Russian gold medalist, skates in the 2014 Olympics.

Judges watch every move a skater makes. They score the moves.

Q How old is Olympic figure skating?

Skaters don't just perform for the crowd. They must prove their skills to two **panels**. The judges on each panel carefully watch each skater.

The first panel is made of five skating **experts**. They give points for every move the skater does. Harder moves get more points. Easier ones get fewer points.

 It was part of the first winter Olympics in 1924. But it first showed up in the summer Olympics of 1908.

The second panel is made of nine judges. They can add up to three extra points for each move. Or they can take away up to three points. It all depends on how well the skater preforms the move. The judges also give points for the skater's overall skating. Then all the points are added up to get the skater's final score.

A judge uses a computer to calculate a skater's score.

Yuzuru Hanyu of Japan spins on the ice during the 2014 Olympics.

Q How long are the short and long programs?

Individual Skating

Whoosh! A graceful skater begins to twirl. Faster and faster he goes. Soon he's spinning like a top! Individual skaters skate alone. Each skater does two events. One is called the short program. The other is the long program. The scores for each event are added up. The skater with the most points wins gold.

The short program is under 3 minutes. The long program is 4 minutes for women. For men, it's 4½ minutes.

The short program comes first. It tests the skater's skill and strength. Every skater must perform the same seven moves. These moves are called **elements**. They are jumps, spins, and **footwork**. The skaters can put the moves in any order. They get a score at the end. The 24 skaters with the best scores get to do the long program.

US skater Jason Brown does a jump in his routine.

South Korea's Yuna Kim has grace and skill. She has won two Olympic medals.

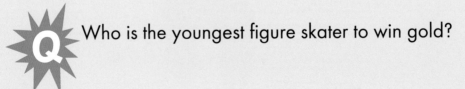 Who is the youngest figure skater to win gold?

The long program happens on a different day. This event is also called free skating. That's because skaters have a little more freedom. They still have to do tough moves. But they can choose which ones they want to perform. This event shows off a skater's grace. A skater also has to prove his or her jumping skills.

 Tara Lipinski. This American skater was just 15 years old. She won gold in 1998.

Pairs Skating

Swish! A man and woman skate together in pairs skating. The skaters are scored on how well they skate in **unison**. The top 16 pairs in the short program get to perform in the long program. Sometimes you see the skaters far apart on the ice. But they are always doing similar moves. Other times they skate close together.

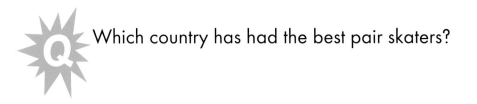
Which country has had the best pair skaters?

Pairs skaters Tatiana Volosozhar and Maxim Trankov won two gold medals for Russia.

 Russian skaters are some of the best in history. They have won more gold medals in pairs skating than any other country.

Pairs skating moves are exciting to watch. One move is the **lift**. The man raises the woman over his head. Sometimes he tosses her in the air. Then he catches her before she lands.

Another move is the **throw jump**. The man throws the woman high in the air. She spins and twirls. Then she lands on her skates.

Lifts like this earn pairs skaters points. Both skaters need strength for this move.

Ice Dancing

A graceful couple glides together. They look like they are on a dance floor. But they are skating. Ice dancing became part of the winter Olympics in 1976. Ice dancers move together. They twist and turn across the ice. They do lifts and twirls. But they don't do high jumps or fast spins.

Ice dancing is a more graceful event than pairs skating.

US ice dancers Charlie White and Meryl Davis do fast footwork on the ice.

Q Who were the first US skaters to win ice dancing gold?

An ice dancing pair has to be fast on their feet. They must do tricky **ballroom dancing** moves. The dances they preform have names like foxtrot, waltz, and tango. The skaters wear dancing costumes, too. You might see men wearing a fancy tuxedo. Women often wear flowing dresses.

 Meryl Davis and Charlie White won gold in 2014. They had been skating together for 17 years!

An ice dancing pair performs two events. The first is the short dance. The pair sticks closely together. They must be touching almost the whole time.

The second event is the long dance. It's also called the free dance. The top 20 pairs from the short dance get to do the free dance. Here, the dancers have more freedom. They sometimes move apart.

Elena Ilinykh and Nikita Katsalapov of Russia skate a ballet-like dance.

Eight skaters made up the US skate team in 2014. They won the bronze medal.

Cheer Them On!

In 2014, the Olympics added the mixed team event. Each team is made of skaters from the same country. Different members of the team compete in eight different events. Skaters compete in short and long programs for pairs skating, ice dancing, and individual skating. Then all the scores are added up. The team with the highest score gets the gold medal.

Jump! Spin! Glide! Twirl! There's lots to watch when it comes to figuring skating. And the Olympics brings out the best of the best. Which men and women will shine? Which pairs will skate or dance to gold? Keep your eyes on the ice to find out!

US skater Gracie Gold charms the crowd with her beautiful moves.

Glossary

ballroom dancing A type of fancy partner dancing that follows set moves; some examples are the foxtrot, waltz, cha-cha, and tango.

element A movement in figure skating, such as a jump or spin.

expert A person who has a lot of knowledge about something, such as figure skating.

footwork Movement of the feet in the form of steps and turns that a skater does one after the other.

lift In skating, a move where a man lifts a woman off the ice while skating; pairs skating lifts are higher than ice dancing lifts.

panel In skating, a group of people who watch a skater and determine the points for each move.

throw jump In skating, a man tossing a woman into the air as she performs a jump.

unison Doing a move together at exactly the same time.

Read More

Hunter, Nick. *The Winter Olympics*. Chicago: Heinemann Library, 2014.

Thorp, Claire. *Figure Skating*. Chicago: Heinemann-Raintree, 2014.

Wood, Alix. *You Can Be an Ice Skater*. New York: Gareth Stevens Publishing, 2014.

Websites

Figure Skating
www.pyeongchang2018.com/horizon/eng/sports/Figure_Skating.asp

TIME for kids: Figure Skating
www.timeforkids.com/news/figure-skating/137696

US Figure Skating
http://usfigureskating.org/

Index

About the Author

Laura Hamilton Waxman has written and edited many nonfiction books for children. She loves learning about new things—like figure skating—and sharing what she's learned with her readers. She lives in St. Paul, Minnesota.